More Flowers Than You Could Possibly Carry

Also by Simon Smith

North Star
LEXICON
Night Shift
Juicy Fruit
Fifteen Exits
Reverdy Road
Mercury
London Bridge
Gravesend
11781 W. Sunset Boulevard
Half a dozen just like you
Navy
Salon Noir

Simon Smith

More Flowers Than You Could Possibly Carry

Selected Poems 1989-2012

Edited by Barry Schwabsky

Shearsman Books

First published in the United Kingdom in 2016 by
Shearsman Books
50 Westons Hill Drive
Emersons Green
BRISTOL
BS16 7DF

Shearsman Books Ltd Registered Office
30–31 St. James Place, Mangotsfield, Bristol BS16 9JB
(this address not for correspondence)

www.shearsman.com

ISBN 978-1-84861-510-6

Copyright © Simon Smith, 2016.
The right of Simon Smith to be identified as the author
of this work has been asserted by him in accordance with the
Copyrights, Designs and Patents Act of 1988.
All rights reserved.

CONTENTS

Editor's Note   11

Uncollected Poems 1989-1990s
VI   14
From *Laura's Lifetime*: 'Hello, hello sleepless'   15
Night Shift 1-15   17
Blink   25
Catullus #117   26

Fifteen Exits (2001)
The Nature of Things   28
Friday, 21st April   30
Red Border   31
Silver Rail   40

More Ammo (1999-2000)
Fairytale Ending   48
The Balcony Bar   49
Spring   51
To Be Continued   52
Bleep Me   53
Outdoor Type   54
Brink   55
Owning Up   56
Clouds   57
Joie de Vivre   58
The Whole Bang Shoot   59
Corkscrew   60
Lookalike   61
Address Book   62

Reverdy Road (2003)

Autobiographical	64
The Magician, Jack Spicer	65
Entry	66
Driven	67
Ideogram	68
[CUT]	69
On Paper	70
South Circular	71
Stealth Fighter	72
Absence	73
No Fault	74
Rainer Maria Rilke	75
Sentimental Education	76
Adam and Eve	77
Equal Footing	78
A Good Job	79
Twin Towers	80
Rope Trick	81
Statue of Liberty	82
Diamond	83
Thought Bubble	84
Orpheus	85
Blue Rider	86
Not You	87
The Day It All Came Clear	88
Olson	89
No Let Up	90
One Moving One Still	91
Me You	92
White Sky	93
Blot	94
Sudden Edge	95
Think	96
Drawn Covers	97
For the Moment	98
Now What	99

Sun Hat	100
Echo	101
Idea	102
Natural Light	103
Instamatic	104
Think Up	105
Apollo Calling	106

Mercury (2006)

Buzz	108
Meanwhile	109
Tee Hee	110
Heaps	111
Who's whose	112
Over the Page	113
Why do	114
Direct Light	115
Fizz	116
On the Instant	117
[Unfinished]	118
Square One	119
Zap Bam Pow	120
Waste Ground	121
Soundtrack	122
Cloud	123
Wow	124
Melted Paper	125
Orange	126
Is As	127
Writing	128
Formal Solutions	129

London Bridge (2010)

On Telegraph Hill	132
Personal Note	133

'Bye, Bye'	134
Martial V 20	136
1984	137
Il Penseroso	138
Oyster Card	139
Honeymoon	140
A Table	141

Content: Poems 2007-2012 (2015)

from [Unfelt]	144
Bob's Jacket	169
Airbrick	170
Ode to David Herd	171
Ode on Human Remains	173
Content	175

again, for Flick, always

Acknowledgements

These poems first appeared in: *Creeping Bent* Winter/Spring 1989 (no. 8); *Night Shift* (red letter, 1991; Prest Roots Press, 1994); *Laura's Lifetime* (GRIllE, 1995); *Juicy Fruit* (Gratton Street Irregulars, 1999); *Fifteen Exits* (Waterloo Press, 2001); *Reverdy Road* (Salt, 2003); *Mercury* (Salt, 2006); *Telegraph Cottage* [with Felicity Allen] (Mindmade Books, 2007); *Browning Variations* (Landfill Press, 2009); *London Bridge* (Salt, 2010); *Content* (vErIsImIlItUdE, 2015).

I offer my grateful thanks to the following for the publication of the poems in this book: Guy Bennett, Jennifer Cooke, Kelvin Corcoran, Andrew Duncan, Tony Frazer, Chris and Jen Hamilton-Emery, Simon Jenner, John Kinsella, Peter Larkin, Joe Lucia, Jeremy Noel-Tod, Richard Price, Peter Riley.

Other poems and translations not included in this selection were published in books, pamphlets, magazines, broadsides and online by: Mary Agnes, Tim Atkins, Charles Bainbridge, Anthony Barnett, Robyn Bolam, Martin Booth, Andrea Brady, Huw Briggs, Ian Brinton, David Caddy, Chan Ky-Yut, cris cheek, Eleanor Cleghorn, Ian Davidson, Lyndon Davies, Dean Farrow, Allen Fisher, Harry Gilonis, Jon Glover, Wolfgang Görtschacher, David Herd, Ben Hickman, Jeff Hilson, Alex Houen, Peter Hughes, Vincent Katz, Caleb Klaces, Dorothy Lehane, Chris McCabe, Anthony Mellors, Rod Mengham, Peter Middleton, Drew Milne, Stephen Mooney, Jan Montefiore, Alec Newman, Kevin Nolan, Kat Peddie, Nell Perry, Peter Philpott, Adam Piette, Robert Potts, Nicole Presentey, Peter Quartermain, David Rees, Ian Robinson, Peter Robinson, Will Rowe, Fiona Sampson, Michael Schmidt, Aidan Semmens, J.D. Taylor, James Taylor, Philip Terry, Tony Trehy, Matthew Welton, Rebecca Wolff. Many thanks to all of them for help and support along the way.

The present publication is made possible by the scrupulous attention of editor Barry Schwabsky, and the patient generosity of publisher Tony Frazer, to both, many, many thanks.

Editor's Note

I've told the story before and I'll repeat it here: I didn't know the British poets of my own generation when I moved from New York to London in the summer of 2001. Shortly afterward, Bill Berkson suggested I get in touch with Simon Smith. Being shy, I didn't act on the suggestion right away, but eventually got around to googling him just out of curiosity. I learned that he had a new book coming out called *Reverdy Road* and was immediately intrigued: Not only do I love Pierre Reverdy's poetry, but having come across the street near where I was living in south-east London, I had written a poem called 'On Reverdy Road.' So I got the book as soon as it came out. It was a revelation: resembling nothing I was familiar with in American poetry despite name-checking Jack Spicer and clear affinities with the New York School's love of speed, wit, and variousness of tone, it had a music I could tune right into, something very much its own though it has also helped me, I think, hear my way into the work of some of Smith's British contemporaries.

Finally I took up Bill's suggestion and contacted Simon; we did a reading together. Over the years our friendship grew, and has continued to deepen even since my move back to New York in 2011. Yet I was as surprised as I was honored that Simon asked me to edit his selected poems. I've carried out the responsibility in the way that suits me best: by letting pleasure take the lead. How could I pass up the excuse to re-read all his books as well as to delve into uncollected or unpublished works that were new to me? From them I have not chosen systematically, but simply cherry-picked the ones that please me most without concerning myself too much how representative or not the resulting selection would be, whether from a technical or a thematic point of view. In this I surprised myself, because I conceive of each of Simon's book as that wonderfully paradoxical theme, a unity of fragments—meaning that I might well have tried to select from each book in such a way as to suggest its shape as a whole. But in practice I found this to be impossible, and have had to content myself with picking out the most striking single jewels in Simon's treasury. In order to understand how his books function, you will simply have to go on to read them whole. One aim of this selection is to persuade as many readers as possible to do so.

Barry Schwabsky

I
Uncollected Poems
1989-1990s

VI

the good eye cultivates the delicate light
streaming through the jewel
to emerge in amber   earthworks cut
the golden light
of paradise a solid   figure end &
source
      from the chalk the white

horse   at Uffington
hovers between thing & function

disintegrating time   a skylark made

invisible

      reaching out
the skilled hands tell the facts

meet in blossom & crystal   this city
of summer & snow   the mirror

the stream knotted   break & grow

from Laura's Lifetime

Hello, hello sleepless.
'You' or 'me' which
'he' or 'she' without
you I walk the streets
and I walk the streets.

The simple flesh I enter
trees and sky studded
the mired networks above,
shoot the long route
to the stars,

and you embrace more flowers
than you could possibly carry.

Your breath flutters on,
not linear more a contour
in air like a rollercoaster.
The tears tear airborne
over the precipice,
each one seeks out
the trophy of you

where our voices carry
and only footsteps remain.
Easily we destroy things;
some people you want
and nobody else will do,
the aimless wind
homing on blowy rain.

It rains all the days
for someone who reads a lot.

Once, deep in the forest
there lived a little bear
shy and unable to speak.
Until the tree whispered
her name she growled
at shadows caged and restless
locked up without a key.

Of course, you can't *write* that.

Night Shift

1.

As generations failed to see *it* coming, survey the plot
or challenge the beast-system, so scions dreamt the gold
while swearing generosity. They've got your vote:
ignore need, encourage want. Cheat. Forget names, the honied
plaudits froth above those Elysian fields, *those*
inner cities a temperate clime, fingers on buzzers & Eden
undone. The sales rep twitters, shilly-shallys by the damp-course
his feelings miscellaneous, the pick & mix of grubby reform.
Amendments, corrected texts, depravity & ignorance almost lyrical
rehearse monologues to embroider separation with myth,
the air between us. Myriad appetites drain the dread citadel;
borrowings, trifles, eroded profit margins the proof,
sharp-eyed monkeys crank hurdy-gurdys sexing leaves with notes,
sample pastures, every square foot for profit, tightening the rope.

2.

The many & various stars, rain-drenched opals
grounded pieces from the crystal night.
Hard coins chafe a mess of tales, chosen right,
letters boxed: for caring *is* profit, & theories accumulate
like dust. Tongue tied, it's all over now, inaudible
on the point of closure the world itself the dark realm.
We want a normal life; you speak down
to us the grand design. Others follow

onto grainy streets, just visible faces loom.
These are humans too, rattling the can. No passer-
by will help. There's an end to it, offer
them up for slaughter, caught,
you see. But the stars expand, heaven netting care
& hope, the voices to be heard by night.

3.

Our land flowers orange, then scarlet
the house shattered. You shelter in its form
raising your head above the gloom.
'Politicians let my people die,' rot

your heart; then clerks shouting oyez through foil masks
toss palliatives & mendacities,
                            stacking doubloons with laughter.
The sale of information sparkles
                    in the dark; choose Baked Alaska
the stalest loaf. That's us, the dim row you needn't ask.

'We're chuffed with the logo'. Collect your pay,
munch a neighbours limb, cashing in your luck.
You count the bonus, skulls shine through the muck,
a *belovèd's crown*, business as usual, you might say.

You pass along the night trench, your progress metered
to enter the crumple zone. *Riot or write* you fall mute.

4.

Thrall to the brutish & the wind's ceaseless trade
the sun is grey for me. Copper follows silver
smothers day for the grubby pence we ventured south
to haul home. I am sleepwalking … spare me
some change, mister, my days & nights are lead.
Someone has taken my place, or might as well have,
pressing the flesh sublime. Sealed with tape, chained
to their gratitude, resolved into knots, that lone, sad

flautist. A migrant device shews up in product
networks, countless stratagems, padlocked breath,
theft to the bone … the northern music

of exile. Across this surface a garden of effects
blooms like mould, across this state security is now
an industry, pressing the blades softly to our mouths.

5.

Banker's foreclose on ranked participants
delayered with packets of Kleenex, their gaps retouched.
These passengers swept from platforms leave no impression:
the stations cleared, the ease of users paramount.
Tickets clipped serve the purpose of motif, trapped
within the given & last payments. They will not return.
And business will not suffer, but trades on their chorus
(the language of crowds) collects their *lustre*: its quiet address.

But do right by the good folk. You must. To hold is to care;
they cannot avoid harm, lapped by the heated winds into controlled
response. Work-tired, they offer all, a bright regard to share.
Their breath freezes to sugared night, to no kind word.
And the brokers, by-products of detachment staring at the wall,
cold players helping themselves define some inner chill.

6.

The mother (her sentence), grasping the notelet of accident
& experiment, files into Personnel: their empty
shoes mere storage. Her life decorates labour
braided, embroidered as speech glitters across the tent:
varieties netting choice; her life mere formality
will run & run. Research & Development gather
the heat in booklet legislation, data correct
field-defined. But rosy contusions spread unchecked:
no word spared expression. The lyric-system takes charge.
The delta of veins magnify her brilliance as day & night converge
& what is held in grit glistens, dissecting rain to mend

at the shared expense bright sensings. Each one runs to her end.
She was found by stories where field-surgeons turn back the sheet,
identify the victim with nowhere to hide or seek.

7.

'It moved me,' the face buried in ice, a lover's
complaint. Letters rain onto the street
picking out the thread, a combination of characters
& us the crossed-gates. *Do you copy?*
Flick the yob: the portrait lifted from masks
of flesh pegs back tradesmen's dreams
their carved lusts honeycomb the cart
& coin the appeal. A bright new shirt.
This homogenised carolling just won't do;
reading the empty journals the wreckage shakes
rattles their mortgaged souls. Stress levels high.
Next stop the hospitality suite. Oval faces
like pennies, dirty tales plugged in the shade.
The face decayed meat, fuck it, I'm telling you.

8.

The reach of desire beyond the neural,
the lark's endless song at summer's edge.
O, I could laugh, warble & win the appeal,
when after rain we walk across the grass:
memory for comfort only we cannot return, of course,
but apply through proper channels, catch the thread
crystalline at heart. That bird, he's a civil engineer,
trembles before the blade of light, pressing the mid-

point to knot the heart & leaf: *this* the pilgrim's share,
who stood great witness, language lodged
in his throat, heard but seen nowhere

to float above the verdure, an airy fugitive ledged.
As one speaks too soon we meet & part,
but there it is, our pilot, 'til we find port.

9.

The carcass takes on personality wrested from the swamp,
his freedom tied back, hands fixed with lard
& twine. Sinews we exquisitely map
the sylvan scene, the crazed Perspex
of his shattered cockpit. Zephyrs over the ridge
balance this cube of light & with the key-pad
purge the system. Greasy stars rehearse the safe percentage
river's web, a shadow surface occluding the hideous muzak.
Under the canopy, 'Bang! Bang! Bang!' Driven home with verve
to reach deep coma: there was no Paradise only *exit
to next concept. Cut at source.* We are the strawmen
inhabited by meanings, the shades with stitched lips.
O, to walk across the grass again, the light's sinews record
the shattered pavilion in kisses & bees laid out in living code.

10.

Oak-framed that oat field: its intricate
map with infinite depth. We inhabit the scenic pull
locate the root, encoding by multiple
efflorescence every unit, any item of fruit.
Like walking into a clearing, clean & new,
like aspirations reflected in silicate, written with rain;
the air hisses a rhapsody of grasses. Shreds laid in my palm
singing the gap: strands tabulate the grain *in situ.*

The valencies of want & plenty were designed out of synch,
won't add up the dust from our eyes; they circle
instead, settle a haze (*rosé*) on silos of grain & missiles:

a science gleaned from rubble, broken apples & flint.
As order *is* love, radiating seed for a crown of grasses,
precisions in salt, galleries of light, many voices.

11.

What-You-See-Is-What-You-Get
reflecting on the gilded carriage human units
attached at the form; roads in bland networks fit
our sovereign's coat. The reactor ghosts the crown like a fist.

The chart starts here & cells divide. An apparition
peeling the foil, he survives to occupy the shell,
offices unlit: bid him sup the packet a future perfect
with sense. Turpentine pours down his chin.

He reads the meter for the frisson of sculpted tint:
the trickster's clouded glass programmed to connive,
'We believe the machine will live'. & it does, star-
labelled, the motto's salt clarity encrusts the beaker's rim.

The king reads off formulae, sampling signs of adversity
from beauteous forecasts & wraps the tattooed fantasy.

12.

We live with our neighbour's radio locked in crystal.
Launched down the echo avenue, voyaged forth
between lips, a sodium flare to guide the cough's thick trawl,
tourist of his own life & the whole sad charade torched.

At least one side of the conversation was entirely lucid
blind as paper sucking us down. The lark's scorched tongue
exposed for flowering. Derangements flood unimpeded.
Dug at the piano, he made a soft quilt of your cheek,

the tattoo – bluish dream-girl – ghostly beneath flesh.
Thus he spake forth the goofy fantasia,
his own tongue called an ambassador to escort the silhouette,
tuning the fetish, prelude to ambrosia.

We smile, things are well & wish the day over again.
Consume the sleeping draught, for the dream lays ashen.

13.

Mutton attests the hit, flaming coupon to the
urban stew, & forgetting our need for drink, or water
rushing over shingle, the rough speech leads to
disarray. It won't amount to much, a little blood from the
ear. *Our hero* notes the glistering firmament (the reason why)
returns the nightmare to the city. Trade our human
enclave for vile medallions, charm the thug to guard a last
dead crater of sky, the broken spell his price.

Mark the eye, its socket lanced, his face
an anagram for pain. That jellied orb
runs down his cheek, a screen of blood. He sang
like a nightingale. Against *that* our communicator howled on &
on, *'The recknynge! The recknynge!'* smiled a grinning
wound, jabbed the dagger & ripped right through.

14.

By night we searched the landscape for lost dreams.
None recall enchanted fields nor soft rains,
but capital confined to crop lines, the restrictions
in birdsong. Tonight the hunt for blood descends
again, assails the tissue webbed with frost.
Famished hordes hunger for atrocity, marbles viands,
their *jumbo meat*, spiced kill astride the spangled ditch,
breath steams singing the pulse as fingers tingle.

Branches pursue the hopeless through thicket & copse,
victims prayerless as vermin who mount greed on blood:
meat stapled to the grid. A brassy trumpet calls the halt.
Beaters thrashing bracken stop. Blue crack at water's brim;
the hunt chases more than harts – to beat darkness,
the forest itself, with flash of red tunic & scarlet harness.

15.

Cloth laid on the grass of common ground,
clean linen. An orange spills its zest,
our breakfast at first light, as the dispossessed
we walk among rootless, homeless, drift around.
These the Innocents wear dresses like tombstones,
lives already posthumous. *Her laundered effects creased,
neat.* Abandoned. *Love* lost in translation *eased
from her child's broken mouth. Common ground*: dream on
loquacious stream relume intricacies of water,
    the plaited chronicles,
as clouds shunt the twilight into valley shade
of desolate architecture, tail-lights …
    our points of reference fade;
we are entering forever a picture untroubled, endless,
dreaming paradise we cross the stile, lengthen our stride
with home in sight & the hard north star our guide.

Blink
(takes #1-18)
    (for John Taylor)

Licence my roaving hands, and let them go,
Before, behind, between, above, below.
Oh my America! my new-found-land!
                  John Donne

Joyous explosions of reds, blues, oranges stretched as far as
                  you can stretch orange!
Difficult unruly father you are, sucked in spat out flecks &
                  spots & stars,
(suspending belief
            cut loose
                      a long haul
                                cracks the code—my
ship rolls over narrative—kissed left off
                              target the heart;
side-step, jab, jab, jab, punch, jab, punch, punch,
                                punch, kiss. First
thought best thought, second, splash cheap red wine,
asks you   tanned and white hint,
                        flesh I spy
your body the stars go berserk for, as far as I can....
"Love" is the word, tipped gold, tipped silver, licked
over pink and jewelled,   tips it over…
                      'Good morning, love'.
Rush—tail-end—one blink   and you're gone.

24th December 1997–27th July 1998

Catullus #117
(takes #1-6)
>(for Bernadette Mayer, C.H.Sisson, Louis Zukofsky,
>Peter Whigham & Frankie Howerd)

>*The schoolboy with his shining morning face on*
>   Tom Clark

Curious to learn how many kisses
at my own cost it is the pleasure to lick up
(three hundred) tomorrow when the shops open,
useless without loving:—never steal kisses! Of all
light-hearted men and women none is
lighter than Catullus is today
(used in imaginable tomorrows)
sharpest of sharp hellebore, flower at the field's edge.

Love me so we'll laugh at all without return,
even if the formal field of kissing
sounds preposterous, sweet as sweet; all right, I'll
bugger you and suck your pricks (the guts melt).
I hate and I love—you may well ask how:
as the fastest piece of timber or the passing plough.

                    10th March–12th September 1998

II

from

Fifteen Exits

(2001)

Things do not connect; they correspond. That is what makes it possible for a poet to translate real objects, to bring them across language as easily as he can bring them across time. That tree you saw in Spain is a tree I could never have seen in California, that lemon has a different smell and a different taste, BUT the answer is this – every place and every time has a real object to correspond with your real object – that lemon may become this lemon, or it may become this piece of seaweed, or this particular color of gray in this ocean. One does not need to imagine that lemon; one needs to discover it.
       Jack Spicer

Wittgenstein influenced me and still does. Lucretius impressed me.
       Emmanuel Hocquard (Norma Cole, trans.)

1. The Nature of Things
(takes #1-28)
> *(for J.D. Taylor)*

> *Mothering goddess, visit my poems also please with your grace*
> *And be with me teacher, lover, and poet*
> *As I undertake to make for you*
> *These verses on the nature of things.*
>   Stephen Rodefer

Dear John, my friend
can I call you that?
No news, but poetry.
Served the cat's dinner,
emptied the bins, then bed.
Awake, sleepless beyond tired
I ate an orange, scratched my arse.
Sandra dreams. Strange, terrible beasts
mean no harm, but she watches the hours,
stories of tumult, ruin and hurricane shriek,
a young child in a woman who lost her body,
she feels the waves lift her arms;
De Rerum Natura rests on my knees.

These coarsened times swallow the Works of the Ancients too.
It took the Nature of Things to fill the Universe
my study no exception, and my Universe.
Great paragraphs of the *Tractatus*
propagate our Lucretius, '2.026 There must be objects
if the world is to have an unalterable form.'
Today they lie beneath the barks of oaks
Love pinned to the tree,
one might transcribe an ounce of pleasure there;
instead, left to dissect brutish facts from valueless objects,
good to nobody but for knowing the limits of poverty
worthless atom after worthless atom,
the nothing gained from nothing;

beasts and birds and fishes—laments
shed over lands populated the seas
to exact the protocol with a terrible Creation
from seed or pearl shocking the five senses.

All I ask, my wife's kiss a sparrow's
chirrup, melody of the little bird
hopping about the eaves. All praise to her!
Let her quicken the earth's axis with her charms,
bring the circle about again
the land under cultivation,
morning rushing to the leaves
funnelled towards this static quiet.

6th–20th April 1995

2. Friday, 21st April
(takes #1-23)
> *(for Sandra Watson)*

> *The world of the happy is quite different from that of the unhappy*
> Wittgenstein

At work you could be anyone,
say there is a God and Christopher Smart the casualty,
the spell quickly broken rattled tender clay
knowing sometimes a casual blossom freshens the mouth
sometimes as beacons cross-country allege a livelihood
caravans queue along the road somewhere.
Now the sun's out I feel happy, as though politics could be Love.
The more serious things get the deeper the bark of wolves is neo-classical,
light fallow towards 8.00 p.m., Friday, 21st April the position
of the sun, wind speed, RPM disposed towards the Gods.

Get up, work Saturday mornings, phone numbers changed
and pipes to be delivered for the last caller;
I sewed information back together, triggered off shiny buttons,
take the flowers and list them as you do a rose no doubt perfect.
Carefree weapons raised bows and spears perishable
accumulation and then not, an assault about flesh peachy or pretty flesh
wounded by cold and bad habits fending off unwanted attentions.

Washing Sandra's back I don't smell to pretty,
the effect is Realism, the way we think;
wings feathered, the Petri dish or sermon
(whether cause or result) fell foul of porcine talents
eating angel cake; the workings out as exciting as the fruits of the labour,
so Love might slip away between the pages of newspapers,
sowing roses row by row the body parts well managed,
No Trespass signs up; this is important news and a relief,
an apple in the palm of sunshine hundreds of miles away,
the indifference of turning the bedside lamp off.

May 1995

4. Red Border
(takes #1-28)
> *(for David Rees)*

> *A slow and stopping curve southwards we kept*
> Philip Larkin

I. Utopia

> *only the hands that touch her as flowers*
> Anthony Mellors

      then one fine day everything exactly
as you've guessed—the
sound Byzantine,
an average weekender on patrol greedy for the stuff
      teethes prior to the feast. My love is a child and a bawd
pulled the knife on me.
Documentaries stroke up a fever 'til my pockets sag. The cabinet
crammed, trompe l'oeil add to torment,
      but no formal suffering I've practiced
my survival technique for the day, deep, deep blue cleared of hindrance.
At Yalta you might, inventing countries nobody ever heard of. Idle hours
      the weight a bluish hue,
sideburns dove-grey dash about the real economy, a price on your head,
      ditched judgments of yesteryear
packed with solar
energy, askance to the gift I regret, the next of kin 50s style
      slumped in a pink easy chair.
It reads like a book but rejects the flavour.
Maybe I'll learn Welsh. Albeit the loops are mine.
True as the wind, true as the rain, as invisible as the blue
      gas hovers above the marsh.

Dirty coffee cup by my feet,
must try harder at the "Night Diary," an oasis to return to. Find/make

        time. 21st January 1996: my fingernails scratched the water,
clean out pipe. Deep inside the main each car's golden distance
        from the one in front.
        The sun floats about the meadow crazy as Whitman.
Codeine does the job good. Make a note to myself. Can't bear
        to look. "Codeine". Debts bite hard. More jobs
will have to go. Lines crackle like a telephone call in danger.

What kind of man lives in the moon, an enthusiast for my invective
        unthought (like the land)
dirty trains to the wearer's knowledge, forewarned is
        immediate breakdown.
What killed the Joker and finished this book?
The doily attached to the Reality-shaped space,
        behaviourists call
a momentary arrest where all kinds of lace-up shoes
don't be modest, don't be blamed. What did you say
in my defence doubles and redoubles ceaselessly.
        Each thin colour floats on
the surface, today no special occasion; sunsets in the mussel shells.
        Light flocks to the march of concerti.

Led Dido blinded by the fire, shy no more,
teeth obvious as white as toothpaste would be makes good her smile.
Homes overlook the stinking canal, stop at the black refinery.
Her promise the charm for good luck at the head
        the whole discomfort
won't allow me to finish. I began life as a piece of cheese.
The terrorists or freedom-fighters
hoard a little black transistor with in-built alarm. A portable secret.
        Richard leant forward and said, *Life:*
A Loser's Manual. That needless artificial leg.
Detectives clutch at straws. *Good Housekeeping* and the *London*
Telephone Directory for Business Services causes one to misbehave,
        good knowledge
made derelict for its bitterness. How many mays
        would you include in a literary work and silence the fleet?

Reason doesn't even enter into it; although the Imagination managed one
brick and the hint at Creation
    rescued a sugary wine from Common Law.
The irretrievable passes my eyes once only
silver foil conserves the heat for its redness, pays for what
    you don't want.
Add on the continual interruption of a Friday night and we've all gone
    home to our families,
the alternatives are as various as they are various, pried from clemency.
    Ingest slowly before meals these raw gifts.
The men and women who lose their hearts.
    Fed bad milk: it didn't happen.
Wouldn't notice the commuters bound homeward and packed tight as green,
    as orange, as grey maggots.
The Philip Larkin Archive we endure for historical time a workman-like
performance established the radio tone as poorly tuned as the lily
    to the day's rest. How different are you?
The iced surface meets the clouds. It's too late.
    Get to know Paris.

I regret style or refrain
the gelatine plates magnify perennials
out of all proportion. By the time I get to it you
    could've and represent my feelings, I collected
the thoughts with the stale bread into the bargain neat
as the red border. Vapour above land dropping away rapidly
    safely airborne.
Now my heart, now my money. Ah! The fragrance, it's Givenchy pour Homme
100,000 fall, and many dead. I work and sponge colours at the tips,
the distress my Bluesaver to Hades is like a milk pan.

The trick is to reject everything,
    almost.
Black loose hair telling tales of fun
my mind across that dirty river with you.
Hull was the end of the line, sunken densely boiling
    too busy to ask the solution.

I prefer my ice-cream a little melted, visit the old town
for something to do. Draft dodging or writing poetry, many
        a free-loader and genuine talent ruined overseas.
My Route Planner to Farringdon, sensitive, comfortable, fin de siècle
Kentucky Fried Chicken to Kwik Fit seeps through the vanguard,
        the ink not as fast as we believe,
fought Mallarmé for the immense cloud and pot of gold. And lost.

By air obvious as paper causes pure functionalism
the sun-bleached door torn off

entry by the fake and you

and at the end a red distress flare

I confess. The waiter did it.

As the day goes by the great narrative fallen down the back
        of a cupboard.
Egos seep at the corner I relish the beast, you know durable
        as a three-month contract
concludes the search and part of
        the orange primeval sludge, a city left to freeze.
I cry a little to write down your name
        exercise the oblique tax, and too many birds
often relics of quotidian circumstance.
The smelly barge moored on the outskirts
        beneath low white mist.

The orange tarpaulin engulfs the black earth of Lincolnshire. A man
attempts suicide, "what have I done to myself." A halt
        along the A1. Dead flat prairie,
desperate to confirm your necessary role
checkout to checkout, the appointment kept or the fetish
        worth preserving to have found the middle-way vanish
and reappear, as if by magic imprints on the fields
        where the snow has lasted, substitute displacement activity.

Poetry asks the same questions as mathematics: for it is I
Apollo who had high hopes for less than the music to scale,
      a personal view, snake lightning the wound is well
in recession, purple heart this season he jogs along the grey road,
the old ideas treasured in his yellow
      Sony Walkman anti-roll
device, waterproof and all, the letters spell out "S-P-C-R
-T" in blue and also the moments of green, but express
a preference for greedy
karma and children you gotta
      work hard or jot down the figures.
Tom Raworth was too hot.
Buy a check shirt or print blouse.
The collage an emergency legend, the cash full of snow hunts out
      the airy culprits overhead.
I like etiquette an attempt to label
      the song cannot travel to the end left to daddy
his left leg is sensitive
to the weather, his bomber jacket has elastic panels,
wears it baggy as the experience of tonal dissonance because it won't
the Pleiades drift above the subconscious
      delicate pigments act;
to strike out alone through the long grass on all sides a maker of paths:
I can really admire that, said the artist's impression like haricot beans
      do, sweep past the rump of afternoon

Move or focus I can't

II. The Age of Reason

> *The Singing head, the different metal head*
>   David Rees

Difficult to maintain a self-impression from the middle profile and enjoy
      the unrest. Nobody really cares the population
      shunted from village to town. Fables to rent.

History as it whistles passed, and how many angels can I include in one
sentence. Forget pinheads—clichés are true and all you take
into the oven. That's not a question but a whirlwind. He lives
      just behind my ear, to loosen
or cope, you must come by now; the bombs put you to sleep,
as experience touches red. The publicists have won the battle:
      small trees frosty, next
we flash through some godforsaken shithole like Grantham.
      Composed of the bits, so ends another pointless year
and marooned by contract I'll dream it for you. Told in the shrug
of the earth, waived birdlime, a question
      did occur: on the Issue of Greatness, only visible
to the naked eye the dead men
carry their debts as far as the Styx and no fringe element,
      the land ripped up
into slag heaps for the local people to afford a homestead with a porch
to piss off. Whilst we're talking emulsify the *Dasein*.
      We want poems about the Subject and I
want my little niche in Literary History! I don't feel well
about the echo, a hangover from the pastoral workstation
      territory formalised. To the madhouse.
Anglers kneel and fish the same water for the same fish. You take
      conventions and then abuse them.
The one thing I always wanted were goats and horses.
I'm collecting poets: c.f. Rodefer's *Answer to Doctor Agathon*,
      his tour de force.
I want to be a goatherd and whip up another cloud of unknowing.
Hindquarters the isthmus, the Palladian mode, inclement at base
      whole flowerbeds look to the sun,
a cocked hat of anti-social behaviours flash celestial, flash Nike
      react odd or even perpetual flight
myriad deceptions, breakneck to dazzle and plan the evening.
      Cooked meats are a favourite hobby.
In this world clones fight colons and Paradise with all debate
      wiped out daunting columns of newsprint and greying debt,
two carriages powered by as many diesel engines lifted from old buses,
      put up your hood or you'll travel poorly

freezing in winter, the beaten opposition
        wrong-footed proves the mess
after sunrise, bright equipment finds you in danger

    THIS IS NOT A SENTENCE

Mitre Square greasy from the centre pencilled in
        a chinagraph scrawl of London

        on the riverbank
aloof, lethal with lime-green
        floats, no touch no sale, rusted books, precipitate
multi-coloured umbrellas. One dead peach-stone,
        the same goes for the single foot-passenger:
the back-to-backs smell damp considering the nice, neat front gardens.
Guilty: reading decadent and subversive literature
        from his shiny Elysian boots.
Shot for paying attention. To what use the yarrow. A local undertaker
walks a tightrope to work with the privileged,
        there's always a job to be done, he says: to preserve
the expression of little selves, a rosebowl wrenching light towards it
        manages your affairs for Good.
        Chough and ibis, at the minus sign. Reliefs swing up, so true.
I don't do fashionably late. On initial impression a personal loan
        made of chocolate. It's fake: the language died
c.1755 and has been preserved ever since in your name, The Angel.
        Descent of the famed, the sentiment of days-gone-by,
I hover in the monstrous distortion happy as a lark
        gliding over tundra/ploughed field/moorland.

As the eagle I am the one who sees everything down to the chemicals.
Grass blades and the wind like us composed of hostile echoes,
help the wild beasts. Exile
        tightens coins in your palm
before you can make a name there, before monies appear in your account.
Headstrong young Freddy checking timepieces in St Petersburg, saving up
        to walk in the countryside; members of the orchestra see

into this man's bloodstream. The only solution to bed
down for another winter surrounded by dictionaries and the love of them.
        Study a family of chimpanzees, you needlessly rock the boat.

"Cariad" factored in, I know unenglished the flavoured Welsh, opaque
bubbles of cold air hang by, cloudy pear-drops of speech,
        a Love Poem I tell you, a Love Poem my sweet,
from Siberia via the North Sea, and for those who died the coldest
        hole in middle air improved no chances,
stars wander joyless thus far
        sure and combustible snapshot creations a trio or less than
chance abandoned, balanced on this momentous wave.
Looking for a poem called 'The Horse,' insufficient evidence
minty with particulates drifting along a dust track
        weeding the hostile camp.
"Out to break the old rules, eh. What do you have pockets for?
        'My Little Wing' to a bygone era.
We can't all be troubadours wandering the highways and byways."
The wind screams gale-force. Easterlies roughly in isobars
strip lights flicker, I'm alive the office building tells me.

Three iron figures stuck to green and brown meadows, King, Queen
        and Knave, the cabinet holds a deck
of playing cards the Ideological jukebox, some kind of
precious retreat smells bloody as the feeder towns north of London.
The soundtrack of everything hurled goodbye, what rhetoric!
Discreet loci in the bad weather: there's the body, there's the head,
        there's the steaming vegetables.
The sculpture/theme park fresh as the concept of village dwellings.
        Chew, then leave it
alone to darkness inside the rough sack

the first roses this morning proof of proof

III. Comet Hyakutake

actor poets prat about in arts labs
Kelvin Corcoran

and the new-found sea. Schoenberg
thought it a packed lunch or the rotten warehouse.
Not if you were the last man alive
or the phenomenon of evil. The streets bulge with angels
and all those wankers from Crouch End who go and watch *Trainspotting*
      thinking it's the real thing. Dart a long way, much to, learn.
A bathysphere half-way down to the ocean floor.
Forgive me my seasonal nosings, Langue or Parole, not sure where
      we are: they usurp the deep blue; let's displace
autobiography by writing it. There it is to one side, choc-a-bloc.
      Another cloud, another dream. What jackass did that
offering all visitors a welcome? The troops are in
and I'm a dullard or a dandelion. Can't tell which,
      the whole deal reduced, as attention off-course
the faltering snow of it, the sentimentalism!
Throw back my goldfish, aching with continued
      resistance cleared out the muck
for Orpheus, what remains of the charm on a more realistic charge
      trumped up, sore throat alien.
How you classify the Enemy is up to you,
a gibbering nostalgia for an avant-garde which never existed, indifferent
      to the little seeds and their viciousness,
finish on time for once, choked with painkillers, insignia deer head.
Dogs chained outside, the pupil to the thief—how can it be,
when your whole personality is a literary conceit the stomach burns
      "finally" is not final,
dodging Semtex and bad coffee, wheels past your next victim. The Ægean
is in fact the Cornish coastline, and the appearance
      of the white egret indicates a worrying trend.
Faded now a mere sketch, the collection of sad and ambitious men
      shelter beneath the motherfucker of all parliaments.
Winter biting off the days in isobars. Eventually I will disappear
leaving Dido

This night will be true, if you open it

21st January–11th April 1996

11. Silver Rail
(takes #1-22)
> *(for my parents)*

The fixed arc is designed to erase

What should we do in the coming white days
                    Michael Palmer

twenty-eight
October was a lie. I itch with exile like the wind

syllables in train to appal or dissolve as one of Ovid's beasts,
all the signs of life working quickly I sought

three
white noise refracts on a brown field

(Lower left panel) my lucky star glows, as shown by the workings in
                                        Mallarméan white

You barter away smelling salts or mints,

            to excuse the choice,

and I choose your words, the prism in the other's camp or envelope
as fuse-wire trembles, (for more
            room and daylight see *Gaeta Set II*)

for protean and far flung chromatic scales condense

and throw away

thirty-four
The weather-girl predicts the future 48 hours or so into your own time

you locate the false prophet, and through the sunny day let it float,
to hold down a second job and pay the rent.

                                          Light bounces off the silver rail.

All this encased in a kind of idyll, or jelly, or amber. I would try and hide
the chart if I were you. The sea was a white, unbroken wing of nostalgia.

We enter the world of cones, rhomboids and crystals

the study of German Romanticism smuggled as contraband,
searing and milky as dawn.

I say a flower.

six
the ghost writer passes through that region of the Isles, what lies out there
                                                 digging snow

digging to cut perfection out of the Big Ideas. A grey tile loosens,
slithers down the rooftop. Lushness of a green field memory remakes
                                                      the head.

A's the letter of your absence, in the limits of song

twenty-nine
Hero staring off to the left a middle distance fifth by fifth
in the untitled grey rain which buries all the atlases and listings of the
                                                           World.

twenty-three
whiteout

forty-one
(a murmur) I'm sorry, I'm so sorry, I thought I'd heard your step among the bullet

                                                                                       points

zero
pencil marks like human hair.

Lucky #7

Biography the heat-generated roar, the white mask things touch.

When a flocked paper would suit where brightness might fall, then you'd have more room and daylight, a massive cloud white, massive which number

Your duvet bears a likeness unarticulated as much as creased over itself.

Window   air   city

to the edge, flinty with detail/liquid flow a theory of colour orchid partly,

distraught I carried my body to the choppy Hellespont

forests of sawdust, a humble spoon or I could lend you my fleece.
Blue chalk outlines the advocate, a real showman or situationist,

twenty-five
rain faltering, cornfields unpack daylight. Inside I mass-produce
or perish, toil in suspension, write one last speech from the upper

                                                                             gymnasium.

                        Blue coat and wrapped up warm 2 A.M.
flat out under streetlights laugh and laugh and laugh and laugh and laugh
and fallen backwards puffs of blue snow and laugh and laugh and laugh
and laugh.

Venus lost her footing worked to death

more like a paintbrush than advice, a scar,
disinherited. Simply reverse the polarity, power into somebody I revere,

a delicious drop to the fairground.

Time now to mow the lawn, my life's work titled 'Hero and Leander'
a calm blue to the upper atmosphere, snow shoveled into great piles

thirty-five
(unclassified) cite works of translation

forged objects shoplifted a few ideas

nothing but burns left (a guest writer writing this down).

we all look in books and it rains
                        it rains everyday

Water spills momentous green putting blue between us, his expression
tucked in, inscrutable as the Gulf of Mexico, the smash and grab of style
my throne and home.

Poem made out of white

forty
His queen enjoys a sunset complete with a search for the real thing;
iridescent tangled as fuse wire the fear of everywhere grainy monochrome
lies,

motor functions cross-hatched for shade (visibility) and safety, veins of lead or gold or a gentle caress, or a sparrow calls through traffic

         Drumming its pure form shivers

Pyramid of the Sun

white acrid smoke

all the colours dragged through the snow move of
    their own freewill about the landscape

    air   sea

    earth

and nights at Tournon

sites to rest

twenty-one
the easy optimism of Twombly's *Suma* (1982) beams away in a monograph;

the colours red knocks into are stars over Teotihuacán buckled with Time,
      metamorphosed space into ball/sun.

eight
Psyche splits, listing any adjectives she likes, like 'feathered' for ocean.

The edged chalked.

    where brightness might fall sunlit relief

plums flopped from the string-bag. The black

searing freeze sticky freeze sticky objects to a laboratory wall

a white wall, the heron flown off

nine
_____

seventeen
scentless as a bled rose, close-by the language machine
lived; its silver teeth chewed the line black and blue

the black lantern, rococo style. Alone and wary I had dispensed with
                                                                                                          technique
the north rain proof of an aleatory event or border dispute

Armies run the idioms, the central argument its words cut and creep
                                                                               under my skin true
or false,   dry rust stuck fast

score and read for improvement and education. Made out of the sea.

one
Is, its particulates describe the folds and tucks of a red blouse and you
describe nothing but the subject where there is none but technique and
games, tricks, lines, plains, solids, melody, silence, music, dark, light
trembling disobedience, jangled all over the skin at all levels through
Time blotted ink, blotted out

automatic reveries took control of my limbs, arms and legs jerky,
but in Hölderlin's best voice the rain's soft thud.

Beauty's fifth column proceeds from a state of general alert,
yellow as the meadow, green as the meadow
                      a murdered sister's body made into a harp sings itself

I sing a flower ruined

formal solutions on Monday afternoons, by a birthmark

                and the space around it

In this example the workings were shown, as in prehistoric times

twenty
white bones scattered on a brown field

five
      Second Experiment: Untitled (Boat) 1991

Baked Synthetic Clay, the same energy loss

interference dampened to the immediate environment

using a 2B STAEDLER MARS LUMGRAPH 100
scissored heat and light as by-products.

            (I scribbled hurriedly "studio notes" over ~~Silver Rail~~)

Today is a story and a clear head.

                        24th October–8th November 1997

III

from

More Ammo

(1999-2000)

Odi et amor

—Catullus

Fairytale Ending

As soon as everything's going to turn out like a fairytale
I offer my hard heart to you in a way you'll never tire of

not in a throw away way, but all you can eat, and there's enough
for both of us to compose the meaningless centre of a name

rubbing between two heads two wrongs to be going on
with although it doesn't make an unmade bed nor a plan
for the day. You do what I say as tomorrow I'll do for you—

however; just yesterday an 'I' or a 'you' pressed to the lips
meant more when you were around the less now you're

not—you make yourself a target playing hard to get
so do what you want, I suppose, and double-back

everything's in a name: the hit and missed body

moves in time you see I can't see for the reflection

the easy way out is to walk in the way you do.

The Balcony Bar

I was dropping down from the office to make sure

you stay here where now is not the time
for looking back Orpheus-like to the one
I simply couldn't take my eyes off. No.
Now's the time to head off for the right

place (we hope), unreliable in the Moderne

sense of now when there's no telling who
knows who's next, but I'll put my mind to it,
a putative sign for sure of the grinding of teeth
and the idle practice of stacking loose coins.

That was the year Eurydice got whacked,
I'd hidden at the top of the stairs behind
the comfort of an amber beer where I spied
you from The Balcony Bar greeting your other—

limbs heated to white-hot
I crave the half-hour with you
he will have not the lifetime
without you still to follow,

and I'll put a bet on you used to complain
there's not a decent man in Town.
But I've already lost it, made the mistake
of my life, looking back at the good times

when you seemed so chic in combat trousers

missing precisely the point, for God's sake,
point-blank, which points some other way

just ahead: we follow the same old cracks
in the pavement which is where I come in

you get rooted to the spot
and about where it stops.

Spring

Red cars are faster than blue cars
white vans cross lanes faster still
to beat the light the Transit once
a chippy's benchmark for cutting up

the inside is now yesterday's van
when compared to the zippy Astra.
Grey clouds rush by the wind stirs
up newspapers in sheets of rain.

Crocuses and snowdrops burst consciousness.
The bookshops, offices, cafés, pubs, banks offer
nothing Sublime to a sweet tooth—it's Spring
and there's something you haven't told me

about wasting away almost all my life the first
thing you do is wake up to the place spoon
and bowl in the compartment next to revolution
and let the crowd wash over. It's a cutting

wind the red ball bounces by not to
dwell on it things jump for no reason
a toothache I couldn't look the clock
in the face cold as the Weissbier

you tune into to your heart's content.

To Be Continued

White camellias rain drops whack out
of shape one petal after the next
drop one on top of the other cued
clouds rush by stranger still then gone

southerly there's more order to dirty pots in the sink

than reason to the weather I re-
materialise there's something
nagging me out of step—Item:
black dinner plate; Item: blue

cup (missing saucer); Item: knife;
Item: a lost teaspoon at bottom
your heart hard won half
there and half not in my head

the washing up across the room waits for me
—bands of light queue the things still to do

Bleep Me

You spit me out the usual excuses I know enough of
to fill both sides of foolscap and cram the margins.

No, I'm not seeking an apology, no I'm not
like that. To love you is to walk slightly to the left

or under the ladder wobble at the heart of here and now
you are empty with one more of your 'episodes,' and it's one

too many: I guess I'll have to put up and shut up.

But I will carry on reading biographies to see if I can get it right

and fall into character when I know you'd prefer me to talk
face up to the wall I know you would unconsciously fall into line

talking to people is part of my job and if you find
that too personal then tough. Take it or leave it

or choke. Don't read this the wrong way I could
stroke your back or rub your tummy, but Reality

is a blur full with each thick moment to the exploded
person. Of course I love you

with all the obscene urgency of a fool:
to love you is to drive the wrong way

up a one-way street and still keep going just as you

Outdoor Type

The lead-grey pencil line is the beach
sliver of silver bow down then up

from my point-of-view emptiness it ain't

it's a heartfelt thing we've been watching out for
you and nobody else in the quick green glow one after
the other blip that jumps over the slow brown fox.

Well trodden gravel sticks to my knife-edge calm
a car park if you can picture it no wind-cheater to check

the storm or fault this third day of August bent
around the entry and exit signs as any number
or years plonk on to picnic tables the way feathers fall
first this way then that along the watching edge.

Outside its so beautiful a day we should be grateful
hidden among sand dunes prickled on marram grass

capsized no ordinary boy who'd be nuts out on the choppy

estuary this petrol-blue afternoon an orange-sailed dinghy tipping

every washed up hull carries a poor soul too far to float free then fold

Brink

The dizzy orange wave in your mint-cool sundress
and the baby-pink hair clips all that useless stuff
sticks in the brain no argument stopping up the air

not for us, no siree, the familiar lipstick-
on-your-collar routines like a wire cage

I can't afford to let you out of my sight

me in an uncontrollable sweat, a victim of stimulants
raindrops keep singing in my head then and only then
you've got five minutes while I'm off to find myself

you drive me mad when I'm window-shopping
with the brown mules you blew ninety quid on
(an extravagance when I prefer sling-backs)

however, I want to make it clear where my blind spot is:
that a woman being the natural sum of her clothes
has not been true since the Medieval period of lovemaking

that the panties I know you are not wearing are our secret.

Owning Up

You smell sweet as a little nut on a hot day
like today repeats itself played through

the radio by the pool a shaft of sunshine
drops in on the bikini that touches where it fits

my idea of fun you kid yourself her folded
note is a meaningless shortlist of dos and don'ts.

Okay, okay, one on one we're of two minds

who else is there but you and me
try and explain why my thought's your thought

while you're at it it's just as though
I've walked in on the end of what do you think

you're doing over and over and enough is enough.

Listen: pretend if you're not meeting someone you should be
in which case I've taken five minutes more than I'm entitled to

and you've gone your way and I've gone mine. What was was.

Clouds

You don't have to look to see so much as

set the record straight, reverse the impression
at high speed a shape lived in feels like the first

time, but what's the use of humming and haaing
to catch up on daylight—why it's a one-way street

with you and about as far away as the song goes.

What am I supposed to do just to get you to notice—

when the time comes the memory breathes
for thirty seconds only yards down the road:

if it happens it happens and the clouds over there

like Denmark and the clouds over here like Crete
and for now the shortest distance between we two.

First things first: when I've a window, maybe kicked off my shoes
we'll look into it, but until then if I'm not in your face I'm off duty

you'll have to barge me out and let go a space you'll have to

Joie de Vivre

Or just get up and walk around enough to show
I don't do rejection all day every day I just get up

I wouldn't would I have known where to put my gaze if I could fritter
some time learning some not I wept for setbacks setbacks impossible

to fix you'd said quietly why why when you quit the minute hand
chops the next minutely then backs up right back to the start

where I belong I know not the like it's a hole not a hesitation
of the sort not seen before or since of course I miscalculated

you scare as easily as I scar when you say when and enough
is enough of this by which I mean one carries one over into

the next self or other woman I see is you jumping out at me

now you're not looking on the badly damaged you won't
come near I serve notice it's a style thing I miss in you the end of

Life and the how-to-be-you-I'm-hungry-for-news-of

humming away contentedly it'll go away is what I have to settle for

the fact we don't know what it is each and every time there's a blow
to the face to face up to the 'special occasions' was too much to ask

you stay burning where my gaze once was

for now you're gone pressing forward
it's a long walk to the beauty I saw

in another's face to see the beauty in yours.

The Whole Bang Shoot

Item: the navy v-necked sweater was the last thing
you gave me with a hint of feeling attached to it—

anchored at the sleeve I recall—and if its your idea
of a joke its lost to me the kind of thing I can't afford

to lose, a power cut coming where it did as optional extra
to how could I have been so wrong as in where

did our love go where our love once was in the air

proof to all unknown centres of the knowing Universe

who warned me you're nuts. I must be. The fact I was
might drag one down by the mere thought which is to live

in a neighbourhood that never was that fashionable now I'm not

looking my best these days now I've collected the whole set
with a side order of olives to pick at now my life's

assumed epic proportions its unbearable to live and swallow
hard and at the same time take a deep breath looking

around for what I don't know but I do know this if you can
fix it which is not to say which is not to say so and not say no.

Corkscrew

You don't understand do you I can't take the pressure with no sign
of nonsense even when you're not looking I'm getting in the way

you know I know you know I know you know I know I drive you
out of your mind and I know that straightens things out. I'm half

asleep not going your way is it lifted out of yourself for the occasion
when life means Life neither forever nor for the first

time sounding the last post while I'm waiting for another
to come along you'll do he thinks she does at full stretch.

Today couldn't go better, could it, but what are you feeling?
I think you think you don't give anything away do you

but you already have so much so my heart could break
and it does now I've let my body go I can't say what I mean

the tail-spin I'm in is getting us nowhere you said
I always love the pretty ones, always have always will:

which means being caught out again and yet again knocked off guard.

Lookalike

You're here in the shadows you wear like your raincoat
worn out through the left elbow I'll wear if you can't you

won't drape your right arm about my waist, but it's fortunate
we fit the same sizes you pull over my pullover, 'moth-eaten'

the exact words were yours I'm in the middle of
the ten minutes there and the ten minutes back

we agree to differ: never take a peek at the Eurydice
sat in the corner, lipstick, mascara, et cetera, never!

Its *Mister* Orpheus to you and lying's my first language
not a fall-back position to the way things are meanings

at least a week old they grow blacker and blacker in your eyes
staring me out you look right into Pluto's old, grey discs

you see your windows are not my windows to peer out of no,
where there's a warning ahead: 'Don't come home tonight, unless

you drink less,' that what's it's all about you and me—Number One.

Address Book

I scout the pubs and cafés and shops but have to settle
for a near miss or your ghost which shows up you

and down I go you can't have it both ways in step or out
you don't arrive at a party all glum-faced now do you with what

you wish or without, if you blew hard enough I'd
disappear a grey comma the common light falls across

the road I try phoning from a phone-box to leave my feelings

untraceable I wish I could but I can't cross you off one less to know

forget about houses, forget about cars let's re-invent libido
written out of what tipped into my lap only to tip out all over

every street wandered down, every flea market visited to escape

your remains remain like *cartes de visite* or 'post-its' reminders I'm in
your head and I want my heart back, thank you, I've an unlucky charm

to drop off at your place the remainder and moral of the story:
not reading the right signals right you end up in the wrong bed.

IV

from

Reverdy Road

(2003)

Autobiographical

To think this entirely autobiographical constantly
looking over my shoulder. Method is my sanity

whilst the others snuffle at the trough clearly marked ambition.
And whilst night visitors arrive in the car nobody moves and nobody

gets hurt, we had wondered where you'd gone.

Mine's the expresso. Helps calm me down.

The Magician, Jack Spicer

Rattled Tupperware can scarcely control my excitement.

The gifts started rolling it up all over again, sent the present
squeezed out of the tube in chain reaction to the kick which

back to back switches the fallback position to fall out
of the blue a light bulb sputters its lack of breath on

cold air ideas in black and white, please, gestures to twist

and stall the angels as they amble up the close, so
close the gate – were you born in a barn too close

by the stable? Kicking their heels—mind how you go there
you go again there you go stalling—all poets are lyres

in the city with a blue edge that laps my front door-
step, so close to knowledge a dimly held view under

street lamps outside the weather defiantly Russian right
off of Mayakovsky's steppes to the bend in the view-

finder. So what do you do you do what you do

do don't you—all or nothing or do it all to the heart
of you, bound hand and foot, and that's what's burst

step to one side then proceed to where you go there
here smiling with all the charm of a Paul Daniels.

Fix me a Jack D. Jack, the impression cuts right away into
you, you knew all poets are liars didn't you, you knew.

Entry

It's 4.17 a.m. I'm motionless the landing
dark. It's 4.18 a.m. you've got one wish
left almost real as the gull-cry flew from your mouth
into mine, you wrap your left leg around my blue
shadow no one-off 'thing' you can cut and paste
your own amusement in the photograph beaming
away, this is our story melting, higher up. It's 4.18.a.m..

Driven

Driving over to your place the twin towers of Crystal Palace
hang in empty air by my neck craning round empty
rooftops the skyline clear and a clean wiped sheet of grey
when you make household gods you cradle civilisation
and I've not found my voice yet, no, not even now clearing
my throat, but I'm glad you changed your mind and decided
you liked the Venus as much as you love dancing
cherry blossom—our love with the shelf-life unknown
I've been meaning to tell you we just get in the car and go.

Ideogram

Yellow light against grey
winds slip through the background
knot to letters the mark the present
pattern fills my head with
all the women I'll never have and nothing
I can do about it but blame
the market place and rhyme
itself myself I can hardly breathe
ideograms by the pound
by the pond a simple chord
repeated. Repeat. Stop. Speak
for yourself report yourself spinning out
of control be yourself and idiomatic
grey seals made of blue-grey waves
to sing, to sign, to buckle under

[CUT]

Pelted with sun's warmth sharp chip hair
sing song cut in a straight line diffusing light
leaves spread the shine filtered down
lime trees I mean London Plane
at random from the dictionary picking
all night the smell of lemon peel binned
words at the end of darkness love shone
primitive roses just white cistus lemony
cloud sun behind cloud closed behind idea
disappe

On Paper

It all seems fine work above
and below eye line white

surf blue water white
noise waves copy

dozens of them salt
mirror broken purple

wounds lap into one
square box of attention

South Circular

Dove grey clouds float about
a railway cutting sun falls

red vixen and cubs sparrows
twitchy fellows flown into

the shine an answer lies round
explanation bends equal facts

sewn into light by a few pence more
unhitch your narrative wagon right here

Stealth Fighter

I'm just trying to keep as low a profile as possible
bouncing off blue rocks cubs and vixen out sunning
sparrows twitchy on power cables little blighters
missing their train of thought you'll have to excuse
the absence of the gods
they have better things to do this side of the fence

Absence

This space should be named after you

No Fault

The emphasis walks right in and smacks you in the teeth

directly proportional to a smack without warning explanatory notes

and the obligatory forms to fill in complete with boxes to tick

Rainer Maria Rilke

You look as though you shouldn't be here
fruit looks right through you to the angel

Sentimental Education

Thank you for handing back the neatly folded memories
thank you yes they were my fantasies thank you

yes they were mine and quite sentimental quite thank
you too you're right of course of course they were

too sentimental and they were mine
all mine and stunningly simple of course

thank you for the thirty boxes of dreams
sentimental full boxes full overflowing

sloping dreams over every side thank you

Adam and Eve

Slalomed of diamond into another place

our newness worn shiny as a badge

the world is what I know when I bite

into it a sign of movement of moment still

to come the air between us

the material hardness of opinion

my heart will not budge neither

heart can budge an inch

I love you filthy feet you know

Equal Footing

I'm standing in for a whole series of values,

emblems maybe until our hearts break or turn

the past we all disappear into voicemail

that blasted waltz one more representation

please then abstraction tailed off too far off

A Good Job

I'm writing *The Book of Competition Verse*.
And after that I'll make a career
move write performance poetry the wagon
I've hitched the people that matter to
a wider audience caught in the debt
loop of my own echo

Twin Towers

The futures are being re-written
there is no return to sender no
Truth to Fortune from which you
spin no position where cold
shadows or way forward where
that voice is coming from
there are figures in the ground
between one world and another
between breaths spot you
with one kiss then another

Rope Trick

Song is policy wherever you are

if you see a gap fill it my love

for you a trick of the light

I too am counting from memory

and toes connecting up

as old rope fill it with love

I try to rescue the dead

straight down we come to

a gap then the weather to gape

the same place as a trick of light

Statue of Liberty

Flip the square to the left
or right 45 degrees and presto
it's all a question of perspective
or a diamond we look in the mirror
and look upon the Dead
image like he dropped dead
leave me car sick bring me
your tired, your poor, your hungry
when all the assembled
missiles are a parody of dream
aesthetic time is over
now in the time of plastic
what is in my bag is what I carry in it
keeps me hanging to the last
page of Life

Diamond

Look in the mirror and look
upon the Dead diamond
looks the same like a virus
transmitted through every
pore and computer in the land
every home what's in my bag
your charm defying gravity
just for laughs is what you do it for
the image left me sick in the car
at the screen and to the core

Thought Bubble

Where once an hour stood

now an idea stands

and the phone rings on

and on your desk now

not one idea in your head

but on a c

Orpheus

The hit was immediate

whatever was doing the rounds

I am transformed from god

to human that's how strong

my love is who did what

to whom and who did not

Hello! With the nothing missed

out

Blue Rider

The pure picture on CCTV
pixel count leaves desire
wanting to burst from my
pants the Mystic Writing
Pad sleep sleep sweet
prince, a cloud is a fractal
so is a poem it's five
minutes to the next bar

Not You

Are you on the 'A' list? Me neither.
No, I'm not a part of the audience.
Nor apart. All ears. Sitting it out.
That's me. All echoes. All the ones
buzz off and gone on. Now. Not me.

The Day It All Came Clear

The point of all those trips to this moment
(day trips) turns the echo about face the echo
rings about face the note off mark buzz
the fact equals the face three down two across

Olson

Looking off the watch-house quay into fog.

Olson scrawling walls and every surface.

Hi, gran pops! Information log-jammed.

Everyday is small. A few drops

the other way look the other way there

it goes the World harder than love. The line.

No Let Up

Phone goes again at the very edge

I tend to use voices myself

what some folks said next to the skin

light burst in on that that leads

to other things, which seems obvious

and I'll miss you forever, and I'm

the most normal person I know.

Did you know that? No, I didn't think

how much like Life it is

getting into bed with you.

One Moving One Still

Check for debris in the moment
unfolding death hand on door
knob the next level rain dots
my eyes your eyes in moving
blue head over heels hand over
mouth goes along and drops off
the line takes one for a walk

Me You

A sign indicates presence down the clear road
the head is directly in the statement
arrow to the field this instant the line
of view unsettled the story of how it all got
started how it all got here place for place
fence to fence rapid change pursuit forward without thinking
past absence or a second glance you stroke
to me

White Sky

Nothing stuck to the surface
won't come over in translation
fills in the box endless cocktails
what fun language in your shoes
glass is glass I think not there
and so we are things pictures
sounds the chicken crossed
the road and no one knows why

Blot

Rain is blue lost and brought back
shadows shrink into objects
this coffee cup, this fig tree, this forget
me not blue and white and unnamed
yellow flowers like paint blotches
do you count scratchings out
or not the cup tips over and leaves
a ring whether you like it
pick up and carry forward
squeeze through. Rain. One moving
off drops silver in broke off
silence no such thing
can't stop it seeing can't stop
the gaze picks up the line and floods
the path at a rush wide sunlit
weather low terraced dwellings
in vivid yellow morning start
here drop the grid looking or running spread over
the most important thing at the time
flat silver blinds are blind
I see my name waits outside

Sudden Edge

In the form of matching wet and cold
this kind of thing flakes off brought in
to light no let up up to the very edge
I don't know when I said it or to whom
I said it to I don't count all this chatter
where it falls shadows fold inside my mouth
shadows fall under my mouth

Think

Continuous string of ticker tape or DNA
images moving faster
ask the usual unknowable questions
mostly chatter cold toast into light mostly
we have erased the surface cold till then
touched by the curtain and the edge
flakes off the vastness out there

Drawn Covers

Crazy pattern to the sky this afternoon
at the moment you walked in a curl
of paper nothing funny just nothing
screwed paper right up close open
both understand handed a riddle
last and lost that's where

For The Moment

That's where we are
to the left and right
silver sharp the throat
get up and see the place
a room how it is about now
endless cloudless sky
this afternoon heads off
to the horizon where signifiers
float freely above signifieds
or endless sunsets or whatever
the moment you like
screw of paper white
windows black windows

Now What

It sounds it
thoughtless
easy easy
takes you to that bridge
calls up the signs to keep
things going we could well
you could x-ray
the title towards me
bounce then plop
plonk that's right

Sun Hat

One plus one equals one these days
I'm getting nervous about what
letter to use next next to what
I need a sun hat as any belief system
where'd you'd end up if you're not careful
screwed down to a plywood squint
and it's you're one hope it's quick a moot
(or is it mute?) point I do loop the loop
God is there too and he makes me nervous
the all-seeing eye with a bored grasp of Reality
the gloved hand seems unnecessary though
a split second and he was gone
does the 'he' always have to be a he the present tense
present boots shiny in the dusk
red sun blue sky green trees white cloud
if the world were that simple we'd have had the answer by lunchtime
as summer air between buildings or a snap of the fingers
shout and an account is opened or slip
out the backdoor heading for Eternity
language takes you to the bridge
and down that road nobody need know
through an x-ray to the title
so that's the decision then plop
it all turns out right in the end like a cupboard
and there's me, ten years from now. Simon.

Echo

That's for you. Not me.
Reality which the gaze bends
into extended thought you don't
know what might turn up
next the bend a sideways
kind reach out from my big
black trench coat it is and it
isn't for you to hold like an Idea

Idea

Make yourself sick with it is one answer. Come on.
Next to touch touch me off
this piss yellow streetlight wipes over day shining chrome
with a rag sun after sign after sun after sign
a blank a crescent and a circle nice fat glass
table felt through it

Natural Light

This is where a shrug gets you then.
Shush. I can't for days between
a cold front passes gleaming sky ahead
rain swept in there I break off
to the left cold and wet white puffs
a work called 'clouds' light gone
from eyes disappeared one way
stop. Or was it that
children in a file marked 'children'
showers grey to touch silvery
light from eyes deflected upward

Instamatic

Thoughts done that in the machine the brain the mind the sequence
dark under bright shiny horizon and gone
I don't know when I went
I have nothing to say except in black and white as a child somebody
not by choice
surface not used but hello in place of a full description
simple as light
pencil is still
water ice lemon
the plan next to the thought fizzy leaving early
could be but isn't on the instant

Think Up

Moving through other things

there is only one way to be without

you one after

think in a straight line

read forward queue like anyone else almost doesn't almost

a photograph squeezed out through

stars first glade opposite policy

too much high-hat too

overcrowded pixel count dot to dot I blink the very edge walked straight

                                                                    into it stars first

cut grass opposite glade or meadow or money

walked straight into the photograph starting with 'go' mirrors step ideas

                                                                     side on tip-top

left umbrella

Apollo Calling

Air flows out

over teeth

on edge you wouldn't know but a god would follows does

writing cheques and poems

gradual unfolding as fluid

gaze is a notebook yes of course I do

fling all the signs there are

curled with paper works life

let's see how far

silvery edge air flows over

in spite of a child's

cry or sax

throw away waves throw away

signs signals children what do you use sidetracked dire

sigh

V

from

Mercury

(2006)

Buzz

The breeze is the note left by the meadow

for me to read hold it up to the blue

it's Real Life down here, you know

it's all right shooting live ammo

through my head things go straight

trapped in a box not the message

Meanwhile

Back to Orpheus' place and the deadline.
Songs fill the World to bursting bursting
from radiators bursting from grass the chord
that is discord played across blue

Tee Hee

Indeed. Stuff.

Wet paint into exact space.

Whatever image title or body's the risk

lips in the eclipse

has it has 'the' has its position

chair against door.

Things are now

the way things are too fast to notice.

A chequer-board of desire

one red one blue one yellow one four-sided

figure not that regular either all closed in

or no such thing exactly in effect mint

the same 'a' indefinitely the same body's

place where bones fit

side-netting pushing out into life

it hesitates

Heaps

You walk sing-song to the shape not who

you think it is though

a closing movement in the way of looking

budge in the other direction makes a note make

a note tipped with your sour kiss as collusion

as collision leaves a signature dissolved to

the next disclosure that's settled then

all traffic stopped next

to the ticket kiosk except blue cars the rest drive on

air steady film a kind of flame flies through

the coffee table to form thought

a letter I'm writing to someone else. Or this

you wouldn't know. End with a little biog

or a hard-boiled egg.

Who's Whose

Echo. Sense of it carries back as a 'hello'.
More polish. What we want. More spit.
For which there is no evidence. Me peering back
steer by other stars. What's that buzzing noise?
Stop it. It's irritating. Spicer's listening in. For which
there is none. Not a mirror. Not a moon.
Not an understanding. Funny little thing.
Everyone knows everyone in this explanation.
Goodbye with your heel. Echo the go.

Over the Page

Not a cloud. Like that. Very like that. But not
suddenly time accelerated and I was gone
no feeling in my legs pearl sky few
moments after silver
air the way ice shrivels before heat the chill
should be here now but I won't go
orders continue to be issued
'it' says more than we believe we believe
the air that clouds the trees
was the way but goes nowhere
not given in a smiley way
ideas side on
solution: walk faster. Quick.

Why do

Dry stones

disappoint wet stones

inspire no excite they can they do I'm not trying anything clever

polished stones from the beach you know

Direct Light

Tight reflection I almost go into and calm down

now I've got the whole of Western Civilisation

pressed behind me surplus to pixels and dormer windows

brighter when open

to air or scissors

leave the tip one

dot

one on icon

lost only to itself you

mirror behind disappears

starts to tip and list lisp twist by

sunlit where that does

you or me sweep end on a

Fizz

That's what—no exclamation marks for you my boy as grey is cold and of white
ceiling above a thin stain
sky cleared of satin light where the sound is skylarks
up and down all day long fills the absent eye blocked open hazel
green as a marble the idea the area small sample a speck
caught sunbeams as muddled as rain
when the sound paper cups blow about
bite through Reason if I can just pull it apart
as soon as field is to sky yellow is to white
counts the sound o to stop it up where it is
on the instant

On the Instant

Where is the sound you can't open

the idea I suppose bit through at the 'e'

pull it away one clean white sheet like summer

mirror to the alias wipes it out no single moment

life is grey

horoscopes are upbeat

towels are delivered with tongs

behaviour is inappropriate if we don't know

where it leads write it out and wait

summer with ice

tap the glass. Hi.

[Unfinished]

And there's more.

Black and white stopped like a photograph

shifting furniture about for the nth time today then lights out

drifting off over the fence and away where the eye can't settle

rain streaking grey laminated panes float in the orange clouds

Square One

WIDER & WIDER
The air is blunt and soft
hammered concepts
until they fell apart
lone damp jackdaw flops down

BIN LINER
Lone damp jackdaw flaps across

AIR STRIP
Lone damp jackdaw touches down
then off that's the first sign
the air is blunt and soft

Zap Bam Pow

Give a false name where I am
in relation to the good there's a light on in the room. I am not alone.
We are happy. The idea is the first time to make a note. Drop in the fresh
air leaves drop grey walls of cloud manufactured warm shade
but there are no meetings scheduled point-blank
the air is blunt and soft push me in the right direction fell apart
I grow wider and wider and wider and wider and wider and
squared we were little dots

Waste Ground

Sunlight dropped on black

funnels young birds intent to look one is winter one is summer

can't be wrong

time of year dash dot dot dot

in the cards hearts of course bleaker

blacker is the measure of

pretty lost join the procession through

the edge

do with your mouth whatever there is to do

with your mouth loss is error sit and watch

without realising it united untied is a way of reading and missing a go

only the ocean this occasion

Soundtrack

Flags are limp and wet the hair like fish bones there's a smile for you we can write these things
down into a kind of memory beyond the limit it was the kind of daft deadpan realism received into dream shadows passing even

Cloud

Beauty is there in the same breath trimmed to a new minute

of stars of feathers or sharp gum Beauty is a minute

the Real is a metaphor for

streams of the personal need not trouble us

within days or even a synapse clicked fingers

throw the top after the empty bottle

who's is the white face echoing T.V.

where we start is where we go

seize that expression one step ahead where the door is misreading is

part of the job

red comes to mind then fades

more responsibility in the grey rain. And then more.

Wow

When Muses feel abused nothing courses through break of reflection
not this one. Not this. Not
why the change of shape immediate arrow thin in air shaped with light
wander in gentle grey morning light but he doesn't know yet
notes, notes, notes. More notes. Voices carrying families, dog-walkers, tourists
centre to the immediate under a thin coat heavy rain pelted the office
                                                                  windows grey air
a long red squiggle, red squiggle, long red squiggle
'Mercury' chalked in yellow where dust particles bounce on or off
                                                                 the grey pavement
cold and real memory is made from the optic nerve feeling not much
                                                                          but the shine

in all directions

Melted Paper

Today blue signifies distance and nothing else

what does 'gel' do

down like rain or fulfilment

touch is a degree of brightness

lick the days clean if you're a cat

like normal people doors are squeaky birds

and this is my 'cat poem' dreaming cars

'a' + 'b' = 'c' and you follow the same path home

Orange

Piles of apples and lemons awkward dim and slow

scents ascend the air to the valid point

like sun spots sans sense and other celestial punctuation

inserted between piles of yellow clutter (light)

are these grey socks yours or mine? Culture sticks in the grey

of an evening in and white noise trips other sorry moments of reference

Is As

The sky and horizon record blue Infinity close by the brown roof tiles
$$\text{of my parents' house.}$$
Always have always will.

It landed there with its capital 'I' and never melted.

Never went away, a clean and dense snowfall the year 1978.

My mother arrives safe as an ironing board.

She walks across the street in front of the mini-mart and is gone.

My dreaming starts, and that is as strong a proof as I know.

Writing

Black and white jumps focus

the same moment it saves my life

the afternoon is strangely grey

saves my life for another five pence extra

promises are a kind of trick that comes true

Formal Solutions

How many body parts tickle at once
there is no getting away from detail
feet drawn under shade
seagulls touch fences then think
better to offer an example
blue raven's wing of a sky further
proof for no good reason finger
tips and needles through
Michelle tippy toed opposite
thought through
thought so thought
about thought once

VI

from
London Bridge
(2010)

all you had to know was the answers
                        Ornette Coleman

On Telegraph Hill

I.

Dornier, Heinkel, Junkers, and ME 110 queue from Calais
to north-west Kent, fast shapes sweep time
delayed piston, thunder, whine over
suburban Surrey, down Sussex Downs. St. Paul's their hub

circling, the swarm begun to storm, big black splashes
darken paving stones, soon a downpour. Black cloud
of Ruskin's nightmare, Denmark Hill to Brantwood.
drrrrum rumrumrum drrrum rumrumrum drrrum rumrumrum

II.

Click. The washing-machine ends its cycle.
Families sit late, sunlit on stripy deck chairs,
heads swivelled up, eyes swimming to the late,
late summer showers, rows of shiny business class

criss-cross sight-lines with flight paths in secret
cross-hairs, feel their way down the spokes and invisible
corridors of power to Heathrow, landing safe as houses.
Out of the airport lobby, the mad dash to the next working lunch.

Personal Note

Let's meet, discuss plumbing, give up phone conferences, be happy.
Pink cloud tinged, a little sunlight to offices, London clays all walks
of human life. I take the opposite view, but no matter. Peeling white
paint, yellow brick houses opposite of unconnected events and concepts,
a series for no reason but the London hum: brick property, bottle the person
not a philosophy maybe, but as metropolitan logic runs deep, easy to follow.

"Bye, Bye"

"Nude descending a stair." Look, another version of it strides by
to reinforce that sense of a journey, a purpose, albeit stutteringly

*

(Drum roll)

*

Buy it out of the box

*

That's my philosophy, 'don't look back,'
the late afternoon light failing

*

The crate of beer rattles down the yard, the years,
and the office workers, where do they go?

*

Which brings me bang up-to-date and the echoed click of the keyboard,
the reminder, the mnemonics. It comes out this way

*

And now to split the atom. Any atom.

*

Picture the scene tap-dancing over cold-cuts

The re-arranging of deck chairs. My back garden under International
Arrivals

*

From the toilet the perfect smell of pink
chemicals fused with cleannesses' moral imperative

*

Drizzle. The ice I imagine.

*

A few short things.

*

For my next trick the fusion of ideas with ideals.

*

On this occasion – occasional.

*

A few more. Short things.

*

250 more grams of Lurpak. 'You are what you eat.'
No longer the myth of youth, or yesterday

*

Or think out of it

*

More importantly, 'where have they been?' Ian Curtis enquires.

Martial, Book V Poem 20

If only you and I, dearest Martial,
could fritter our days endlessly idle,
if we discovered free time, "The Good Life",
ignorant of big houses and "Big Names",
or the boring laws and their dusty courts—
no, for us: bridle-ways, chatter, the baths,
the Virgin's Aqueduct, bookstalls, the shade
of urban gardens, drinking in "The Sights",
the gymnasium – our daily routine.
But the state-of-play is neither's got it,
the good times sinking down as each sun sets.
So every day we loafed, chalked up as debts;
wouldn't every man live, if he knew how,
giving it all away to here and now?

1984

Air in space of a wing and profit for proof do the work obviously
and us hapless apes count the lovely big coins and our stars,
dirt under nails, a mess of layers, like to unlike for the eight-hour stretch.
The point of seeing metaphor, ah, the responsibility,
responsibilities old and new run freely as the water
to dissolve and change names, reappear all around—
one lone sparrow on the line.
The stars being of human flesh beside my future
landed on the doormat
the quarter-light projects fields to sky
for which there is no interior philosophy let alone an answer
next to light gurgles and runs out of the drains.
Stark as that.

Il Penseroso

I don't want this to turn into a showcase for Michelle and her friends.
Finches peck in a clockwise clockwork movement.
If you want to know, I come here to drink, perhaps helps me start early.
On the corner Michelle re-materialises heavy as a fly, uncharmed by
                                                      your charms—
the speckled wave: metaphor for our two voices the eyes pecked out
but the notes survive a lukewarm twelve minutes in outline of the shrieks.
The very next day clouds float above power cables
for now a sparkled wave stands in too—
dissolves me into many ecstasies, which leads one to ask
where's the coincidence, in what endless seamlessness?

Oyster Card

'Cummin Up!' is the eatery of choice on the A2, the one for me.
I see the world from that porthole, scoffing chicken wings, chips, a Coke.
The buses are regular, pillar-box red, and the drivers happy,
sometimes not. It's all a bit of a lottery that business,
where you can't predict outcomes.
Never was that good managing the guesswork.

There are distances travelled though the gaps
between tyres and curb remain fairly constant.
Journeys, trips: a dirty white container truck
(foreign plates), neatly behind a bendy bus
whisking an OAP 250 yards up to the fork.

Her GP supplies comfort and pharmaceuticals.
She was wearing a navy coat, Burberry shopping bag,
can't remember the rest, but the artic is probably
Central European, Czech, Hungarian. Polish even.
Heading our way up the Roman road to the Midlands, up west.

Honeymoon

The bath you arise from clean as a goddess.
Swathed in white and a big smile to boot
crowned turban-like, towels wrapped about
you flappy corner tucked in
at the armpit worn like a mini-dress
the bruised and blistered toe
descent from the mountain zigzagging up
the argument signed off all discussion under black
clouds, all the sing-song hills zipping along
commands and questions, 'sing if you're glad
to be gay, sing if you're happy this way…'
and the deep 'V' of your cunt below….
First tea, then a mug full of chocolatey coffee.

A Table

Out of the woods and into history. Talk above, discourse below the oak. Table legs thick as a maid's, no one day without a conversation above beeswax polish above a shine.

There once was an oak tree and it told stories. One of those stories is this table, and lives were framed. My grandfather was a fireman on a steam locomotive, which disappeared into a tunnel. On the other side of the hill he was a train-driver, 'choo, choo'. He smoked like a train, then he died. This made my mother sad. I didn't know mummies cried. Now all the mummies cry.

My grandmother wore a floral apron. While my grandfather stoked his train, she fed the iron-black coal-fired range. On Mondays she washed all day, and so hard all the furniture popped out into the garden.

The table occupies the same space, reflects the same light it occupied and reflected circa 1920 when it was made, not by craftsmen, but by a machine process to look like it was hand-built.

The table I'm writing on is like a microphone. I'm reeling this off from the knots and grain of amber wood.

Genuine oak, fake skills.

The table proves the passing of time, and paradoxically, the synchronicity of time. I've just bruised my left hip, challenging the theory, knocking into its bevelled top, as I slid on to the upright dining chair, one of four that match, and start a lunch of baked beans on toast I'd purchased earlier this morning from the supermarket. Now the meal is spilt, lunch not quite begun and not quite finished.

VII

from

Content: Poems 2007-2012

(2015)

from [Unfelt]: A Poem in Forty-Four Parts

1.

It is a new work with your mark on it
Cut up into little stars – diluted with rain-water
No-one *thinks* like you
That about the child

How one writes & writes over & over the same thing!
But day by day the same sun rises, … over & over & nobody is tired
That I should have forgotten you or so remembered you
This morning's letter here – I will go sit presently

And walk it back to its senses
Held up in *that* light
I to whom they are sun, air & human voices
A promise of pure gold, & thank you, as pure gold

I could not bear to have words from you which the world might listen to
And walk, walk

2.

Dearest, you are the best,
A very, very, *very* "little lower than the angels!"
Thursday is our day, I think
It is easier to say 'thursday' on monday than on saturday

I cannot distinguish between your acts now
The actual good you get out of me,
May be stated at about *two commas
& a semi-colon*, you on the other side

I cannot, cannot
You might have said one word
What do you think I have been doing today?

You are kissed whether you feel it or not
The written thing with a shadow of meaning stays
I should not reconcile myself to your picture

6.

Take my – last words I ever shall *send* you
It is part of the horror of such things
The words "at once," taken out "virtually"
The inevitable horrors of dirt and roughness

Nothing can be done, nothing effectual
My time is out, too much, & too out of place
So free! So free as a matter of pure reason
Poor world—it is more desperately wrong than I thought

Yet the chance (as chance) seems much the same
"Here be proofs"—the system operates beyond
The limits of its operations, quarrelsome letters

As I choose you are wrong & if you are wrong,
How are we to get it right, we all look to you
Instead of opening the door & keeping your secret

7.

I would just *call the police*
Promises & vows may be foolish things
For the most part it is so wet & dreary
Do you not see? … & think of you … do you not feel?

All your corrections are golden
"Little circle" to "circling faces"
The postman fell into a trance
A little, little less thought

To conceive of things, which nevertheless are
Do you smile? & will you "take aim" this time
First of all kiss me in as few words as possible
Is "society" a thing to desire to participate in?

Men who "live" only in the first instance
Next, men who attend to the world first.

10.

Deserve to know, in a sense, "read by your light"
I listened for the footsteps … the footsteps of my letter
Always, always! Yet you cannot, you know, –
You know you cannot for knowledge for more

Reasons than one there was sunshine for you
For you never to have seen my face
'In the city' I seem to have more need
Than usual of seeing you, how can you,

Seeing so much, see that "possibility" ever
Arise in me to you I am wholly yours
In the matter we refer to I am growing

Conscious of one or two repetitions
The words are words, and faulty,
Inexpressive, or wrongly expressive

12.

I want the love at one life's end
In the ordinary chances of life
Two "great lights" to rule the day & night
I write without waiting & looked, and looked, & looked

I like the note beyond the imagination
Tell me—I was going to write *that* "Tell me"
The window being wide open, I walked straight to it to shut it
The shadow had a sign of you I looked after it till it vanished

Now the black intervals
I believe and want not 'proof'
Have you a pair of scales like Zeus & me?

With respect to the immediate
We breathe together, understand together, know, feel, live
"Not to go out in the open air"—

16.

I have the whole effect in my memory
Distinctly to throw away such beautiful work
Out of the window into the dark as if the words
Were too near, for the speaker to be so far

It is always when one is asleep that dream-angels come
The poorest brown butterfly
Will seek out a brown stone in a gravel walk
The thinnest of gauze canopies crowning delight

Your last note for a particular purpose
Why the *wrongness* … dear as the *rightness*
The contemplation of the others

First on returning to them that adorable spirit
In all these phrases phrases which fall into my heart
Who was giver altogether and who taker

19.

A characteristic piece of news your note
Only just comes the knock & the letter
But when you say now you do
Not part with feelings to wear them out

You are likely to care for the sight
As much after years as at first
To talk reason in the face
You are the best of all

Did I tell you once the best thing
Falling as they do on the mere *asides*
May is just here, beside
The truth of days, and days after them

You might have stayed ten minutes more
As children of light so it is as well to say

22.

When you play at threatening without a particle of affection
To bear the weight of the "feelings" there is sunshine—
But the wind continues. Nothing but law & love in them
That mysterious pleasure we have: in listening to echoes!

You stand on the side of the hill and listen
The very pleasure of it all is in the repetition
At the same moment with this *your* hesitation
At trusting in miracles that I never for one

Moment cease all that seems removed from me
Fruitless speculations how to give you back
Your own gift what you say to this little familiar

Passage in daily life detected a certain shuffling
Movement my instinct—instinct—instinct
Thrice I write and thank my stars

25.

I have a raw astonishment I open my eyes
Astonished whenever the sun rises in the morning
As if I saw an angel in the sun in loving me
& lifting me up I see the dancing mystical lights

Which are seen through the eyelids
They looked to me like an epigram
I have written, written, & have more
To write let me be silent as on other

Occasions I take all, because, because,—because
& send you the thoughts which are yours
Now you are talking, now you are laughing
I was *pure of wishes* flow back wave upon wave

I am to forget today, I am told in a letter
Like a reasoner of the lowest materialist

27.

The sun shone almost oppressively, – but now – all is black
I must go and answer … and now I cannot answer it
And do, for the future, let it be otherwise
When you are kept in London

Let the vow be kept by one line
The second dear letter comes close in the footsteps of the first
& the sun was shining with that green light
The very essence of the leaves, to the ground

& if I wished so much to walk through the half
Open gate along the shaded path
I put both my feet on the grass
The standing under trees & on the grass

We shall walk together under the trees
All those strange people <flitting> moving about like phantoms of life

28.

& only you . . the idea of you . . & myself seemed to be real
You may love me for my shoes
You loved out into the air
Is it *eight* oclock, or *three*?

Your flower is the one flower
By this letter's presence thro' the half-
Opened gate and under the laburnum
"One day walking by the trees together"

In spite of that felicity to remember
To remember and feel *this*
As vividly, as now

Siren island to go out into the open air
So as to continue a full thirty yards
From you and the tower

29.

A noise that you will not be able to call me
An 'effect' in the midst of it all, I took a long breath,
& held my mask on with both hands
I shall expect ever so much teaching, & showing

This thing & that thing, which never were mine
The walk did me no harm.
You are the end of everything . .
So long as I find *you!*

Who left a card
While your roses
Finished steeping themselves
In garden-dew

I do not for a moment doubt . . hesitate
One may falter, where one does not fail

30.

About unknown tongues & a seven year
Eclipse in total darkness I am seized
And bound! the sun is warm, and the day
The vile wind most vile

The more I need you the more I love you
And I need you *always*
Shut up Shelley, and turn
Aside from *Beethoven*

Only it should be *told* and not written
Let him go to the full length of the sentence's tether
Did not say briefly "yes" or "no"

Who came yesterday & left the packet
& came again today & sate here exactly
Three hours ground down in the talking-mill.

32.

Which is a noise I am always forgetting
Help me thro' the gloomy day with a light!
Feel my way in the dark and reach to-morrow
Without very important stumbling

I should hate life apart from you
I could not believe in "love" nor understand it
My year's life spent in this knowledge makes all
Before it look pale and all *after*

Nobody was obliged to seek proof
Of it *out* of his own experience
The worst thing of all is to look back
On times of standing still,

Rounded in their impotent completeness
But you know, of this & all things

33.

I understand, feel & the more I live, not *'the less'*
But the *more*. And for *the less*, . . we never will return
It is too late for a difference *there* . .
How shall I think of you

Drive in the park near the gardens
The gate of the gardens, & feel
You are inside! I shall remember
Our first day, the only day of my life

The only day undimmed with a cloud
You will not see me tomorrow,
Remember! To win a thought!

With this day expires the first year
Short of absolute sight and hearing
Love of the whole human race combine

34.

The bare permission to love for "a return"
Raised me above my very self, on looking
Back in comparison with all the world
All words are foolish the "course I have taken,"

Somewhere among the stars . . or under the trees
The Hesperides, I should keep away from myths
& images, & speak the truth plainly
That you have lifted me, & of life,

Last year at this hour! Rounded itself
To "the perfect round" that first letter
A miracle *between* the knowing & the loving
The secret aloud the character of the letter

I had borne the sonnet like a hero
Mr. Browning is with you

36.

What must you /have >think/ of me
The letter through the book corners
The full sense *collects* itself
So I will go and think over

It in the garden, and tell you more
In the afternoon *my* poetry is far
From the "completest expression
Of my being" let me write one

Last poem this summer as I walked
In the garden just now it is no moonshine
I was walking today what a summer
Sense in the air & how lovely

The strips of sky between houses
I am thinking & feeling this return

37.

Into life in the place of memory now if I am
To live it must be by other means
Having something to say about one
Precise thing. Such things are on the road

As for my walking fast knowing what that
Flower is, knowing something of what
That flower is without a name this ideal
Rises to the surface & floats like the bell

As surely there as the flower
Which admits of shifting personality
& speaking the truth still

Having made your own creatures
Speak in clear human voices besides
After having made your own creatures

38.

Power /of>&/ & sweetness of speech
The mark thrown /away>off/
However moist with the breath
When he sees the *lips move.*

Eyes to see in a reflex image
How these broken lights
Look strange & unlike
I stand by the complete idea

Guessed a little
Now let us have our own voice speaking
When you walk with me under the trees?
B: A: is, to take

Petrarch & Alfieri are the only foreign poets admitted
Criticism, swept back to the desk from the magazines

40.

Derange your 'myth' the sun shone
Autography in the shop-window
Your little note was a great delight
Follow the good news of the walk

If I *could*, by some miracle, speak,
But my life to take and direct,
At this moment only *pro tempore*
Enough to get up a revolution about

Show me how to get rid of you.
The green under green & feel
The green shadow of /it>the/tree!
The difference of the sensation of a green shadow & a brown one.

The materialism of Art that love 'lost'
In the new world all the dim light

41.

It is all out of my head, now, for a moment
All bright things seem possible
When your note came the natural vibration
One more day—one

The literal truth of history I feel you in the air
& the sun but not in detail everything is at once
Too near & too far enough to make me tremble
Quietly as we are, you at New Cross, & I here

I want forms, /words>ways/, of expressing
Being under a charm you are on a hill
Above me where I cannot reach your hand.

Out of the myths we are near enough
The oldest painters painted one, 'This is a tree.'
I live quietly now I *did* understand the question

42.

To the letter, the iota ... open the eyes
Mask-wearing for another year suffocating.
This for *me*. No room even for tears.
Being an angel the simple experimental question

. . the short note, not the promised one . .
This writing upon the question first looked
You in the face walk rather with men
Than with angels! Could not be but that

After all, after all—talk, and indeed think
To prove very, very little . . and I danced
Birds singing loud and the day bright & broad—
A thick mist lacquered over with light

I shall not try to walk out in the heat even today
Statues have more power over me than all the pictures

43.

I settled myself in the corner of our omnibus
A passenger to Greenwich! Last night's rain,
And this comfort of cloudiness
Now, listen. I was not too tired to signify.

You made the proposal about New Cross
An omission of an ordinary form of attention—
I mean to say the great object. As it is.—
The present circumstances greatest thing within the compass

The project into immediate this instance
Looking steadily at the subject
Your own views are—voice to voice

& scarcely do they carry out my meaning
In every imaginable way all will be well
In every point the certainty of hearing words

44.

Let us go quietly away to live the days out worthily,
In particular stop at such an idea
Nothing shall be said of it now delight
At all times letter-communication

The proper word in my mouth is
This burning dazzling morning.
In all things & ways to the last available moment
All movements, seem easy in dream-life

Let us both think—in all of you—
There is just one meaning to all my words
Knit them into the web!
Some words to that effect

If I had had the shadow
The 'obscurity' when I talked of the light

Bob's Jacket

No one barges their way to the front and rescues two thoughts and an odd fly,
as Nina Simone warbles, 'I Want Some Sugar In My Bowl,' off the jukebox.
My guard, my guardian, my page of notes, my jottings…
Is it me or is the whole world prone to blackouts and bad feng shui? It's me.
Sun blooms on yellowy London brick, warms the touch with a blue flame
mid-afternoon (and the ozone up there, a thinning twenty-five mile layer)
and all those blue and brown notes dance along the black and white keyboard,
the secret things of morning sunlight faded then slid down the beer
                                        garden wall.
This warm light and wobbly reason writes a line and gets a life,
so I rise to my feet and leave. The jacket left draped over the bar stool,
the two thoughts and the odd fly impossible to translate.

Airbrick

blinds tilt light into the room

seeking both pattern and procedure

the spray of rain   the space of rain

the space of rain

a white shirt that fits as a white van speeds north

and a brace of green parakeets circle the park

time enough to adjust the shutter speed

a shock of emerald

holds it there

bar coded and it's only Tuesday

misses the camomile calming effect

you are talented as a razor

Ode to David Herd

now is now: we're all commodities in this sense of ending

where reportage meets montage meets collage meets assemblage

to achieve the simplest of things, running, clean water, say

as words

are the angels, the storyline

out of the mouth,

                collapsed on Peckham Rye to conjure angels

as Blake did

at the top of one's voice the lyric

                              causes you to believe

you were there, once   the lyric moment

or something to know by the alphabet or rote, extract

the cento from the heart switched on

talk mode or attack mode? From the dialogue you turn

the next page into the interrogation room

the rate of acceleration of New York is not the same

                          rate as London

which is more up hill and down hill,

and best walked backwards   'I first recognized art

as wildness, and it seemed right,

                            I mean rite, to me'

for an instant, bright and sharp then blown away the clarion something as difficult as

the distant

the meter running of the everyday

alive to the voice of Simon Smith

                                        I'll mail you the chronology

where we were in 1975, where 36 years ago is 36 years ago

when you were my music

you were my music of the spheres my belle my Bau

delaire my round tush my email my Facebook soup

de jour my kind of private dick my Madame

Butterfly all these years gone

by through you

we compare notes

we meet, shall I come

to you or will you come to me

unhappy as Mercury in our shape-shifting

as we row backwards always backwards rolling

towards beginning with all the inevitable permanence

of the concrete breeze blocks, their presence, their weight

their grey bulk

floats off

above

city

air

to be with

Ode On Human Remains, Dedicated to Chris McCabe

                         from the dream read without understanding
one gets one's mind around Blake
and poetry is made of everyone and a glass of water
is a form of being   the air   waves
         in single file
counter   to chance

text you a donut   handheld off
colour and all the charm of a parasite my heart
can't stand   to the end of the earth to the end of error
to the end this goes no further
free rein   to accept the offer or die
of a (literally) broken heart
we no longer live in the age of Personnel, but have passed
directly to the age of Human Remains
when in the end we are all tired of that world
of antiquity where the motorcars look like antiques
in the age of 'e' equals 'm' sea squared tips up the hinge
         of a dull grey
November Eleventh 1918, the full-grown men

return as though they'd just been born
the memory falling

into email

press the 'send'

button at dusk

all done with smiles, birthdays, management, the taking of life,

and the thesis a procedure through assemblage for the next

$$1000 \text{ years}$$

'til then

Content

Like a child I don't like the hard bits, which are good for you

add the metaphor to the mayonnaise & voilà a prawn cocktail

& the hare leaping from your hat is the reason why this happens

& why I've started to like you, you with your eloquent ink

reading this now, this already-history

fresh layers of emulsion & gloss

the rain thumping down, the rain turning

chilly, & why I've pulled the door to

a morning of unending cups of tea from where I stand

at the dormer window, afternoon light reaches out

from my feet & felt hat without confinement

in the direction of 1973

one blue summer's day evaporating breathless

divided into offices

this is a period of transition

what can't be done in one

like a trick where thought expands

the quiet in the distance

& not a foot wrong or a poor habit

& the days pass without comment

www.ingramcontent.com/pod-product-compliance
Lightning Source LLC
Chambersburg PA
CBHW022117160426
43197CB00009B/1062